5 Minute

Self-Care

Quick Tips for the Overloaded Professional

By

Zachary D. Martin

Summary

Welcome to "5 Minute Self-Care: Quick Tips for the Overloaded Professional" – a concise yet powerful guide to self-care tailored for those with demanding schedules. In this book, you'll discover simple yet effective self-care practices that can be completed in just five minutes, whether you're at home, in the office, or on the go. Each chapter focuses on a different aspect of self-care, offering practical techniques to reduce stress, enhance mood, and boost overall well-being.

Table of

Contents

"5 Minute Self-Care" is your go-to resource for quick and easy self-care practices that can be accessed and utilized in just a few minutes. By incorporating these simple techniques into your daily routine, you'll invest in your health and happiness, enriching both your personal and professional life.

Take a moment for yourself today and every day after today and embark on a journey of self-discovery and self-nurturing. Your well-being is worth prioritizing, and with just five minutes a day, you can cultivate a greater sense of balance and vitality in your life.

5 Minute Self-Care

Quick Tips for the Overloaded Professional

Chapter 1
Intentional Breathing

Pause for a moment, inhale deeply, and feel the immediate shift in your mindset. This simple act has the power to completely transform your day; your week; your year. In this chapter, you're invited on a journey to explore powerful breathing exercises tailored to reduce stress and sharpen focus under any circumstances. Lack of concentration can happen at any point during the day; especially when shifting your brain on and off for different, sometimes unrelated subjects. You have the power to eliminate your own brain fog. Prepare to discover the profound impact of intentional breathing and unlock its power within your daily life!

Deep Breathing Exercise
Begin by finding a comfortable seated position, gently closing your eyes. Inhale deeply through your nose, allowing your lungs to fully expand, then exhale slowly through your mouth. Repeat this pattern several times, each breath deliberate and unhurried. Picture each inhale infusing your body with calm and relaxation, while each exhale releases tension and stress.

Counted Breathing Exercise

Sit upright, maintaining good posture, and close your eyes. Inhale deeply through your nose for a count of four, filling your lower abdomen with air. Hold your breath for another count of four, feeling the energy rise up your spine to the crown of your head. Exhale slowly through your mouth for a count of four, envisioning the energy cascading down your body, releasing any remaining tension. Repeat this cycle, focusing on the rhythm of your breath and the sensations it creates.

Body Scan Exercise

Once again, find a comfortable seated position and close your eyes. Begin by centering your attention on your breath, inhaling deeply and exhaling slowly. With each breath, mentally scan your body from head to toe, noting any areas of tension or discomfort. As you identify these areas, visualize sending your breath to them, allowing them to soften and relax. You may choose to silently repeat words like "soften," "release," or "let go" as you exhale, enhancing the relaxation response.

Incorporating into Daily Practice

Invest just a few moments of your day to reconnect with your inner self through simple yet powerful breathing exercises. No matter where you are – be it your home, office, or on the go – these practices are designed to effortlessly integrate into your daily life, delivering substantial benefits. Commit to the practice of mindful breathing and observe the remarkable difference it makes in your overall health and happiness.

You've now unlocked three effective breathing techniques designed to mitigate stress and enhance your focus, empowering you to stay calm and collected throughout your demanding day. By adopting mindful breathing as a daily ritual, you take a significant step towards improving your physical and emotional well-being, regardless of your surroundings.

Take a deep, purposeful breath and begin this enrichment toward self-care and exploration. Remember, the key to transforming your existence lies in the simplicity of your breath – utilize it consciously and witness its extraordinary ability to bring you closer to serenity and vigor. The gift of intentional breathing is literally LIFE, itself.

Chapter 2

Movement Breaks

Exercise holds the key to unlocking an array of potential health benefits for both the mind and body. In this chapter, we'll explore the scientific evidence supporting how movement breaks can positively impact your well-being, while providing simple exercises that require minimal time investment.

Effects of Movement Breaks

Prolonged periods of being sedentary, which is common in desk-bound professions, have been linked to an increased risk of various health issues such as cardiovascular diseases, type 2 diabetes, obesity, stress, anxiety, and depression. Even if you're not stuck at a desk, but in the same position constantly throughout the day, is a risk. It is challenging for professionals to avoid these health pitfalls due to the sedentary nature of modern work demands. However, incorporating regular intervals of movement throughout the workday has been shown to counteract these adverse effects, highlighting the importance of mobility in maintaining physical and mental health.

For busy professionals who struggle to incorporate the minimum suggested 30 minutes of exercise per day, integrating movement into their daily routine is critical for mitigating health risks and enhancing well-being.

4 | 5 Minute Self-Care

Strategies such as setting hourly movement reminders, opting for walking meetings, using standing desks, and utilizing lunch breaks for exercise can break the cycle of physical inactivity. These efforts not only contribute to physical health but also improve mental clarity, creativity, and productivity, serving as a foundation for a healthier, more balanced lifestyle. Remember, most great ideas or breakthroughs occur when away from the problem.

Benefits of Movement Breaks

1. Improved Cardiovascular Health

Moving your body throughout the day enhances cardiovascular health by boosting blood flow and reducing inflammation.

2. Increased Metabolism

Regular movement breaks can elevate metabolism, enhancing the body's ability to burn calories efficiently.

3. Reduced Stress and Anxiety

Movement breaks alleviate stress and anxiety by releasing tension and triggering the release of endorphins, the body's natural mood enhancers.

4. Improved Cognitive Function

Engaging in regular movement breaks has been associated with enhanced cognitive function, including heightened focus and attention span.

Simple Movement Break Exercises

1. Desk Stretches

While seated, extend both arms overhead and reach towards the ceiling to release tension in the neck and shoulders.

2. Walking

Take a brief walk during breaks to boost blood flow and alleviate stiffness. A short stroll around the office or outdoors can be rejuvenating.

3. Chair Squats

Stand up from your chair and sit back down slowly, utilizing your leg muscles for support. This exercise strengthens leg muscles and improves circulation.

4. Wall Push-Ups

Position yourself facing a wall, place your hands on the wall, and lean forward while keeping your body straight. This exercise enhances upper body strength and promotes better posture.

Incorporating Movement Breaks into Your Day

To optimize productivity and well-being, establish a daily routine that includes movement breaks. Consider these strategies:

1. Set Reminders

Use alarms or reminder apps to prompt break every hour or two, ensuring regular physical activity.

2. Find a Buddy

Partner with a coworker or friend to take breaks together, offering mutual encouragement and accountability.

3. Take the Stairs

Opt for stairs over elevators whenever possible to incorporate more physical activity into your day.

Give your mind and body the rejuvenation they deserve with movement breaks! Whether it's enhancing cardiovascular health or sharpening cognitive abilities, prioritizing regular physical activity can significantly enhance your overall quality of life. Start small, with just a few minutes of light exercise each day, and experience the profound difference it makes in reducing stress levels and enhancing well-being. Embrace the opportunity to move, and discover the transformative power of regular breaks throughout your day!

Gratitude Practice

Begin a transformative adventure with the art of gratitude at your core. Cultivating a mindset filled with appreciation and heartfelt thanks can dramatically alter how you view life, transforming challenges into chances for growth. In this section, we'll explore effective, easy-to-apply methods to harness the powerful vibe of gratitude, making sure heartfelt joy becomes your steady guide on your life voyage.

1. Benefits of Gratitude Practice

Unlock the transformative power of gratitude and reap its myriad benefits for your body, mind, and spirit.

2. Improved Well-being

Gratitude practice is associated with increased happiness, life satisfaction, and overall well-being, fostering a profound sense of fulfillment.

3. Reduced Stress

Cultivating gratitude promotes relaxation and reduces negative emotions, offering a potent antidote to the stresses of daily life.

4. Increased Resilience

Regular gratitude practice strengthens resilience, enabling you to bounce back from adversity with grace and fortitude.

5. Improved Relationships

Expressing gratitude fosters deeper connections and empathy, enriching your relationships and enhancing feelings of connection.

Gratitude Exercises

Try these each or a combination of the below exercises to start experiencing the effects of gratitude:

- **Gratitude Journaling**

Dedicate time each day to reflect on the blessings in your life, no matter how small. Capture these moments of gratitude in a journal to cultivate joy, love, and hope with each entry.

- **Gratitude Meditation**

Close your eyes and open your heart to the abundance of blessings in your life. Connect deeply with feelings of gratitude, allowing them to envelop you in warmth, love, and appreciation.

- **Gratitude Visualization**

Take a few moments to envision a moment of profound appreciation, whether from your past or anticipated in the future. Immerse yourself in the feelings of joy and delight, allowing gratitude to illuminate your being.

Incorporating Gratitude into Your Daily Life

Infuse your daily routine with the power of gratitude to cultivate a life filled with joy and appreciation.

- ## Morning and Evening Reflection

Begin and end each day with a moment of gratitude, acknowledging the blessings that enrich your life and imparting a sense of purpose and gratitude.

- ## Focus on the Positive

In moments of challenge, shift your focus to the positive aspects of the situation, seeking out opportunities for gratitude and growth.

- ## Express Your Gratitude

Share your appreciation with others through words or gestures, conveying the impact of their presence in your life and fostering deeper connections.

Gratitude stands as a powerful catalyst for transformation, especially for those dedicated to self-improvement and entrenched in the bustling world of professionalism. By weaving brief, deliberate moments of appreciation into the rhythm of your day, you extend an invitation to a more serene, joyful, and fulfilling existence. Whether you're navigating deadlines, balancing responsibilities, or pursuing personal growth, allow gratitude to enrich your journey. Unlock its profound impact to illuminate your pathway toward an enriched life marked by deep contentment and abundant success.

Chapter 4
Self-Compassion

S elf-compassion serves as a powerful gateway to fostering greater love and kindness towards oneself. In this chapter, I offer guidance and insights on how to cultivate a journey of understanding, patience, and acceptance through nurturing self-compassionate practices.

The Importance of Self-Compassion

Embracing self-compassion paves the way for inner peace and resilience, empowering you to navigate life's challenges with strength and grace. As life continues, its role is to provide challenges for us to conquer and grow. Therefore, if we desire to continue moving forward, those challenges will always be in front of us and inner peace will be our armor.

Developing a Self-Compassionate Practice

Here are some practical tips for cultivating a self-compassionate practice:

- **Loving-Kindness Meditation**

Dedicate time each day to immerse yourself in loving-kindness meditation. Envelop yourself in the warmth of your own loving thoughts, reciting mantras such as "may I be happy, may I be healthy, may I be safe, and may I be whole and at peace."

- **Positive Self-Talk**

    Monitor your internal dialogue and challenge any self-critical thoughts. Treat yourself with kindness, as you would a cherished friend, reframing negative self-talk with gentle and encouraging language. When a thought comes to mind, from yourself or someone else, recognize it as the opposite of what you desire for yourself. Name it as the lie it is and claim the positive, opposite that you desire to experience. For every one time you hear the negative, speak the positive three times.

- **Self-Hugging**

    Embrace yourself in a warm hug, whispering words of self-affirmation and acceptance. Allow your love to radiate from within as you affirm, "I am worthy," "My efforts are appreciated," or simply, "I am enough."

The Benefits of Self-Compassion

    As you cultivate self-compassion, you unlock a realm of potential and blessings, accompanied by numerous benefits:

- **Increased Self-Awareness**

    You will deepen your emotional connection with yourself as you reflect on your thoughts, feelings, and behaviors.

- ## Reduced Negative Self-Talk

  Harness self-compassion to combat self-criticism and reframe your self-perception with kindness and understanding. The more positivity you hear and feel, the less room there is for negative thoughts.

- ## Greater Inner Peace

  Embracing self-compassion paves the way for inner peace and resilience, empowering you to navigate life's challenges with strength and grace. As life continues, its role is to provide challenges for us to conquer and grow. Therefore, if we desire to continue moving forward, those challenges will always be in front of us and inner peace will be our armor.

Incorporating Self-Compassion into Your Life

Infuse your daily life with the transformative power of self-compassion with these empowering tips:

- ## Set Daily Intentions

Begin each day with a loving intention to extend kindness and compassion towards yourself. Verbally promise yourself, to love yourself.

- ## Practice Self-Compassion Breaks

Pause in the midst of your day to nurture yourself mentally, physically, and spiritually. Take moments of self-compassion to replenish your well-being.

- **Surround Yourself with Support**

Surround yourself with individuals who inspire kindness and compassion towards you. Seek out those who offer love, guidance, and support, fostering an environment conducive to self-love. Be mindful of sycophants and those who are people pleasers, catering to your ego. Those who support you are able to deliver to you the truth with a loving tongue.

Cultivating self-compassion is a liberating practice that fortifies resilience amidst life's ebbs and flows. With daily dedication, your capacity for self-love will flourish, enabling you to navigate challenging moments with grace and understanding. Embrace this powerful path into your heart, for it holds the key to unlocking greater peace, joy, and acceptance within yourself and relating to your individual circumstances.

Chapter 5

Mindful Moments

In the intricate mosaic of existence, moments infused with mindfulness possess a profound ability to shape our lives. Taking time to immerse oneself in the nuances of the here and now opens a door to enhanced clarity and intent, elevating our sense of awareness and being in the world. This chapter offers an exploration into the transformative potential of weaving mindfulness into the fabric of your daily life, complete with contemporary insights and actionable strategies for incorporation.

The Essence of Mindfulness in Daily Encounters

Adding mindfulness into our day-to-day life helps we reconnect with ourselves. These quiet moments give us a break to just step back, look around, and really be in the moment. From deeply experiencing the act of breathing to appreciating nature's beauty or the mindful release of stress during daily routines, these practices enhance our overall well-being, mitigate stress, and enrich our connections with others.

Techniques for Mindful Living

Adopting mindfulness can be as simple as incorporating these accessible methods into your routine:

• Mindful Breathing

Pay attention to those stressful or anxious moments (including the minor) and notice your breath. Is it a calm breath? Is it rapid? Carve out brief intervals to be in tune with your breath, noticing the feeling of air moving in and out of your body. This simple practice can serve as an anchor of calmness in the midst of life's tumult, fostering a sanctuary of peace within.

• Mindful Eating

Elevate eating to a practice of mindfulness by truly being present with your meal. Relish each mouthful, acknowledging the array of flavors and textures, and honor the web of life that brings food to your table. Don't just take the picture, let the image of the meal connect with all of your senses and observe them.

• Mindful Activity

Engage in your daily tasks with full attention and presence. Whether it's the act of walking or doing dishes, fully immerse yourself in the experience, letting the sensations ground you in the vibrancy of life. When your mind drifts to a situation or something outside of the present moment, realign your focus and regain your mindfulness.

The Impact of Mindfulness on Well-being

Recent research underscores the myriad benefits mindfulness brings to our mental and emotional health:

• Stress and Anxiety Reduction

Mindful practices serve as havens of tranquility, cutting through the noise of our busy lives and fostering a state of calm and rejuvenation.

• Enhanced Overall Well-being

Regular mindfulness practice is linked to increased feelings of joy and serenity, encouraging an enriched engagement with life's moments.

• Strengthened Relationships

By deepening our own awareness, mindfulness naturally extends into our interactions, enhancing empathy, compassion, and connection with those around us.

Integrating Mindfulness Into Your Everyday

To infuse your day with moments of mindfulness, consider these practical steps:

• Allocate Time for Mindfulness

Commit a few minutes daily to engage in mindfulness practices, rejuvenating your mind and enhancing clarity.

- ## **Mindfulness in Routine Activities**
  Transform everyday tasks into opportunities for mindful presence, bringing depth to the most mundane of actions.

- ## **Create Mindfulness Cues**
  Surround yourself with reminders in your personal space that nudge you back into a state of mindfulness as the day unfolds. These could be inspiring quotations, symbolic items, or even set alarms acting as gentle cues to pause and engage in mindful reflection.

  By dedicating just small pockets of your day to mindful practices, you foster a powerful habit that not only hones your stress management skills but also deepens your relationship with yourself and others. Immerse yourself in the art of mindfulness, and watch as every facet of your life begins to flourish with a new-found sense of clarity and appreciation.

Chapter 6

Unleashing the Power of Momentary Self-Care

In today's whirlwind lifestyle, finding time for self-care can feel like an unattainable luxury. However, the significant effects of devoting merely five minutes daily to our own renewal demonstrate these instances are not simply frivolous extravagances but essential practices for sustaining our balance. These simple acts of self-care—be it through a series of deep, mindful breaths or a brief reflection on the day's blessings—harness our inner strength, enabling us to stay rooted in the face of life's opportunities.

The act of prioritizing our well-being through self-care is akin to discovering a hidden superpower. Grounded in extensive scientific research, the practice of self-care is a verified strategy for diminishing stress, boosting energy, and fostering positive changes that ripple through all facets of our lives, from personal connections to professional endeavors. Now is the time to tap into this understated source of mental clarity by allocating more resources—time, attention, intention—to ourselves.

It's crucial to set aside moments each day for self-attention, a fundamental component not of luxury but of survival in our relentless world. Far beyond simple pleasures, self-care is the linchpin for decreasing stress levels, amplifying productivity, and cultivating a life of balance, satisfaction, and progress. Make your well-being a daily priority to nurture ongoing development and joy.

The path to discovering an effective self-care routine is deeply personal, inviting a process of exploration and customization. This tailored approach ensures that the practices you adopt resonate with your unique lifestyle and values, elevating your ability to care for yourself in the most fitting manner. In the domain of self-care, one size does not fit all; personalization is the hallmark of truly impactful self-care strategies.

Despite the demands and pressures we face, remember the power lies within us to momentarily step back and nurture ourselves. View self-care as an enriching expedition, one where sparing just five minutes daily can unlock vast reservoirs of well-being, happiness, and resilience. Delve into the world of self-care as if it were an exhilarating quest, and you'll find that these dedicated moments of introspection and care profoundly enrich your life's journey, every single day.

By acknowledging the substantial rewards of investing even the smallest amount of time into ourselves, we affirm the notion that prioritizing our self-care is not just beneficial—it's essential for anyone, no matter how packed their schedule may be.